Basi‹

MW00937385

For Breakfast, Lunch, Dinner & Snacks
By Lewis Haas
©2015

Basic Vegan Recipes

For Breakfast, Lunch, Dinner & Snacks

June 7, 2015

Copyright ©2015 One Jacked Monkey, LLC

onejackedmonkey.com

ISBN-13: 978-1514271346

ISBN-10: 1514271346

Additional contributions by Emma Cogan

Disclaimer

Although the author and publisher have made every effort to ensure that the information in this book was correct at press time, the author and publisher do not assume and hereby disclaim any liability to any party for any loss, damage, or disruption caused by errors or omissions, whether such errors or omissions result from negligence, accident, or any other cause.

This is an informational guide and is not intended as a substitute for medical or professional services. Readers are urged to consult a variety of sources such as their medical doctor, dietitian or nutritionist. The information expressed herein is the opinion of the author and is not intended to reflect upon any particular person or company. The author shall have no responsibility or liability with respect to any loss or damage caused, or alleged, by the information or application contained in this guide. One Jacked Monkey, LLC, and the author are not associated nor represent any product or vendor mentioned in this book.

Grab the

10 Best
Vegan Recipes

That Are Cheap, Quick and Easy to

Make...FREE!

"The 10 Best Vegan Dishes" has just what you need to satisfy your appetite, to spare your money and to save you time:

- 3 Awesome Varieties of Breakfast
- 4 Different Delicious Lunches
- 3 Distinct Dinner Dishes
- Many tips and notes to get the most out of every dish
- Options and alternatives for some recipes

Have you struggled with finding GOOD vegan recipes that are easy to make? Are you needing to find recipes that are tasty AND cheap?

With 10 vegan recipes and a number of options and alternatives to some of the dishes, you will have plenty of vibrant, flavorful meals that will fill you up, keep you healthy and looking forward to your next meal.

Get this book FREE

Go to http://eepurl.com/bfE46z to

get a free copy sent to your email

Table of Contents

Introduction: Everything but the Brown Stuff

When my good friend, Jack, was four years old, he wanted a hamburger for his birthday, or hangabur as he then called them. So, his parents ordered him a hamburger at a restaurant, cut the burger into small pieces, and gave it to Jack.

Jack took a bite and immediately made a face. Apparently Jack told them, "I like it, but I don't like the brown stuff."

In other words, he liked the bread, tomatoes, and pickles, but the meat had to go.

When people ask what I eat as a vegan and if I find it limiting, all I can think of is how much brown stuff they eat. Or beige. Or white. Really, think about how little color is included in a meat-eater's diet! Omnivores could have a beige bowl of cereal with white milk, a beige turkey sandwich on white bread with white mayonnaise, and some more brown stuff for dinner with a side of white mashed potatoes. It does not even sound that unordinary until you stop to consider it. So, when asked if I find a vegan diet boring, limiting, or troublesome, I always mention how colorful even the simplest of vegan meals are! In fact, I can't think of a single dish in this recipe book that is solely brown, beige, or white.

In my experience, when people think of a vegan lifestyle, they focus on the exclusion of animal products. When cooking, however, the focus should be on the inclusion of so many other vibrant, colorful food options that vegans augment their diets with in place of "the brown stuff."

Vegan recipes are creative, colorful, and they tell a story about the person who cared enough to exclude products reaped from harming other beings. As Bruce Friedrich of the animal advocacy group Farm Sanctuary explains, "Every time I sit down to eat, I cast my lot for mercy, and against misery - for compassion, and against cruelty. Every meal becomes a prayer for a kinder and more just world."[1]

Just ask Julia Child; all good recipes books also tell a story. Recipe books have overarching themes and follow a specific chronology. The themes for this book are:

-Vibrancy: I'm talking about vibrancy in two senses. First, a plant-based vegan diet is naturally full of color. Items like sweet potatoes, purple cabbage, beets, and spinach naturally create beautiful dishes. Vibrancy is also found in the vegan's attitude towards their lifestyle. I hope this book makes veteran vegans rejuvenated and new vegans inspired by the possible concoctions at their disposal.

-Manageability: Most of us have limited time to cook and limited budgets to spend groceries on. Many of the recipes in this book take under an hour. Likewise, the vast majority of the recipes in this book use everyday, inexpensive ingredients that readers will likely already have.

-Adaptability: While I love olives and kimchi, I realize that other people do not. Therefore, all these recipes are written to maximize flexibility. Tips and suggestions throughout the book will be given to aid readers.

The book's structure is simple. Each chapter focuses on a type of meal or kind of food. The books covers: breakfast recipes both warm (i.e. oatmeal) and cold (i.e. chia seed pudding) varieties; savory recipes for snacks; tasty salads for any meal; soup and stew recipes to warm you up; quick and easy vegan sandwiches; excellent entrees for lunch or dinner, available in grain-based, nut-based, soy-based, legume-based, and vegetable-based meals; and some healthy, low-fat vegan desserts. Lastly, the book wraps up with further tips and strategies for vegan cooking.

As Julia Child would say, "Bon Appétit."

Breakfast

Warm Breakfasts

Pumpkin Pie Oatmeal

This recipe will keep you warm and toasty on the coldest days!

Ingredients - Makes 1 serving

1/2 cup dry oats

1/3 to 1/2 cup canned, unsweetened pumpkin

1/2 to 2/3 cup water or non-dairy milk (I prefer almond milk for this recipe)

1 teaspoon nutmeg

1 teaspoon allspice

1 teaspoon cinnamon

1/2 teaspoon vanilla

1/2 banana

1. Stir the dry oats, pumpkin, liquid, and spices together and let sit in the refrigerator, preferably overnight. This step can be avoided all together, but the flavor profile is stronger when you let the oats soak.
2. Then, place the oatmeal into a microwave and cook for roughly 1 minute and 30 seconds. (Or you can cook on the stove if you would like).

3. Chop up the banana into 1/4 inch slivers.

4. Place the bananas in the oatmeal and then let the oatmeal cook another 45 seconds or so. This will warm the bananas up.

5. Remove the bowl from the microwave. Mash the bananas into the pumpkin oatmeal with a fork. The banana provides a natural sweetness.

Picture inset: Variation on Tofu Scramble[2]

Southwestern Tofu Scramble with Guacamole

Brunch for non-vegans is often synonymous with eggs. Vegans can still enjoy the velvety, savory scramble by substituting eggs with tofu. The additions and adaptations to this recipe are endless. Some of my other favorite tofu scrambles are:

Spinach, Portobello mushroom and Soy cheese
Curried tofu scramble (Use gram masala, turmeric, chili powder, chickpeas)

Ingredients for the Tofu Scramble - Makes 2 servings
1 package (16 oz) firm or extra-firm tofu (Softer tofu scrambles into mush)
1 tablespoon coconut or olive oil

salt & pepper to taste

pinch of cayenne Pepper

1 tomato

1 bell pepper

1/2 cup chopped onion

1 teaspoon cilantro

Instructions for the Tofu

1. Let the tofu dry out about a half hour before using. I place the tofu on a plate and then put a paper towel on top of it. I then put a heavy object on top of the tofu to drain some of the water out. You can buy a tofu press, but this technique works just as good.

2. Place 1 tablespoon of olive oil on skillet. Let the oil warm on high heat for about 30 seconds to 1 minute.

3. Turn the oven to low-medium heat and place onions and bell peppers on the skillet.

4. Once the onions and bell peppers are browned a bit, add tofu and tomatoes and continue stirring. Add spices.

Ingredients for Guacamole

1 avocado

1/2 lime or lemon (1 tablespoon)

Salt and pepper, to taste

1. Open avocado by making incision lengthwise. Twist to split the avocado in half.
2. Remove the seed and scoop out the avocado into a small bowl. Mash the avocado with a fork.
3. Add lemon juice and spices to taste. I don't add anything more to this guacamole as I want the flavor profile from my tofu scramble to stand out.

Option: You can also serve this with whole-wheat toast or brown rice.

Cold Breakfasts

Vegan Banana Split

Who says you can't have dessert for breakfast? This is a quick, filling, and refreshing breakfast to have any time of the year.

Ingredients - Makes 1 serving

1 banana

1/2 cup of plain, unsweetened coconut yogurt (also, you can use almond or soy yogurt)

1 cup of mixed berries of choice

1 tablespoon of chia seeds or 1/4 cup nuts of choice

1 kiwi

1. Slice open one banana length-wise and place in bowl.
2. Scoop out a generous amount of plain yogurt onto the banana.
3. Drop roughly one cup of berries on top of the yogurt. I prefer raspberries and very ripe blueberries, but it is up to you.
4. I also like to add one kiwi. I usually slice the kiwi up and place it with the berries. Finally, add some nuts or chia seeds for a bit of crunch.

Enjoy!

Picture inset: Cup of Chia Seed Pudding[3]

Mango Chia Seed Pudding

Ingredients - Makes 1 serving

1 mango (There are many types of mangoes. I prefer to use the sweeter mangoes like Tommy Atkins for this recipe)

1 tablespoon agave syrup

1/4 cup chia seeds

1 cup almond or coconut milk

Instructions

1. Combine chia seeds and almond milk in bowl
2. Let the chia seeds and almond milk sit and chill in the refrigerator for at least 6-8 hours. For best results, let it sit overnight.
3. Take it out in the morning. Slice up a mango and add a bit of agave syrup on top of the product.

Picture inset: Frothy Green Smoothie[4]

Green Smoothie Bowl

I make smoothie bowls all the time in warm weather. It is, and isn't a smoothie. It is a smoothie because the base ingredients and final liquid outcome resembles a smoothie. However the numerous toppings that go onto the smoothie bowl make it more like a cereal. Instead of milk, think of a smoothie!

Here's a basic recipe for a smoothie bowl:

Ingredients - Makes 1 serving
Heaping handful of spinach
2 Frozen bananas, in large chunks
2 tablespoons vegan protein powder
1/2 cup non-dairy milk
2 teaspoons chia seeds or flaxseeds

3 dates, pitted and chopped

1/4 granola (keep reading for my recipe for oil-free granola!)

1/2 cup berries of choice

1 tablespoon shredded, unsweetened coconut

Instructions

1. Combine spinach, non-dairy milk, bananas, and protein powder in a blender and blend until smooth. It will be a vibrant green.

2. Pour the contents into a large bowl. The following steps are my favorite part of this recipe as the end result can be quite beautiful.

3. On one end of your bowl pour 1/4 cup of granola.

4. Pour your mixed berries and pitted dates (which should be coarsely chopped) beside the granola.

5. Next to the berries, add the chia seeds. Sprinkle unsweetened coconut on top. You can drizzle Agave Syrup on top if you'd like.

6. Mix it all together, or enjoy all the ingredients separately.

Small Bites & Snacks

Hummus

Homemade hummus is cheaper, tastier, and better for you! It also happens to be incredibly easy to make. Just a few ingredients is all it takes. This book contains two versions of hummus: roasted red-peppers and black olives. I also tend to use a little oil as possible in my hummus.

The base ingredients for hummus are:

Garbanzo beans

Tahini sauce (made from sesame seeds)

Garlic

Salt

Juice of one lemon (2 tablespoons)

Olive Oil

Ingredients for Hummus - Makes 1 serving

1 can garbanzo beans

2.5 tablespoons tahini sauce

2 cloves garlic (use less if don't like garlic)

2 tablespoons fresh lemon juice

salt and pepper to taste

1.5 tablespoons vegetable broth or water

Instructions

1. Put all items in a food processor and puree until creamy and thick.
2. Taste-test and adjust garlic or salt and pepper if needed.

Instructions for Roasted Red Pepper Hummus

1. To make roasted red pepper hummus either use one cup of store-bought roasted red bell peppers or make your own.
2. Include about 75% of the roasted red peppers with the rest of the ingredients and puree in the processor as explained above. Reserve part of the red peppers to place in the middle of the hummus.
3. To roast the bell peppers preheat oven to 400 degrees Fahrenheit
4. Cut in half and cook on one side for 20 minutes. Then flip the red peppers and cook on other side for 20 minutes.

Ingredients and Instructions Black Olive Hummus

6 oz black olives

Place the majority of the olives in the hummus

mixture and turn on the food processor. Let the mixture coarsely chop and spread the olives throughout the hummus. I like to leave the olives somewhat chunky and coarse, but this is up to you.

Picture inset: Vegan Granola[5]

Oil-Free Granola

I use granola as a topping on my yogurt, nice cream, over salads, or as a snack by itself. You can mix and match any ingredients to fit your taste buds. Granola is naturally high in fat because of the nuts that are included in the recipe. Thus, I try not to use too much oil in the baking process.

Ingredients - Makes 8 serving

2 cup rolled oats

1/2 cup pecans finely chopped

1/2 cup almonds sliced

1/4 cup cranberries

1/2 cup chopped apple

1 cup chopped dates

1/4 maple syrup or agave syrup

1/3 cup applesauce

3 tbsp flaxseed

1 teaspoon cinnamon

1 teaspoon vanilla

Instructions

1. Preheat your oven to 400 degrees Fahrenheit. Set aside a baking sheet or two with parchment paper.

2. In a food processor finely chop almonds, pecans, and flaxseed. The items should still be coarse. Just a few spins is all that is needed.

3. In a large mixing bowl combine all the dry ingredients. In a medium sized bowl mix together the wet ingredients. Add the food processor items and wet ingredients to the large mixing bowl with dry ingredients. Mix so the wet ingredients all mix evenly thorough out. Make sure you do not include the fruit. You will add the fruit towards the end.

4. Distribute the ingredients evenly across two baking sheets. Cook for at least 45 minutes. Shake up at 15 minutes intervals so no one side of the granola gets burned. You can put the fruit in after 40 minutes.

5. The granola is ready when it is golden brown.

Note: The granola may be somewhat soft when you take it out. This is normal. It will harden as its cool. It will continue to firm up over night.

Picture inset: Kale Chips[6]

Fail-Proof Kale Chips

I've had tried many times to make kale chips only to have them end up either: a) burnt or b) shrunken and mushy. Needless to say, neither of these outcomes were particularly appetizing. Trial and error brought me to the recipe I am now sharing with you all. Enjoy!

Ingredients - Makes 2-3 serving

1 small bunch of kale

Up to 2 tablespoon olive oil (It really is quite necessary for this recipe. Make sure it is spread evenly over the kale.)

1/2 lemon juice

1/4 teaspoon salt

pepper to taste

1 teaspoon garlic powder

Instructions

1. Rip the leaves from the stems and then rip the leaves in half. The stems are quite fibrous and bitter, so I wouldn't suggest including them in this recipe.

2. Use two baking sheets if necessary. You do not want a thick layer of kale. A thick layer will lead to some kale being overcooked and some under-cooked. Give the kale some space to breathe.

3. The trick to kale chips is to keep the baking temperature low. This requires patience as it takes longer to cook, but in the end it is worth it. Try 275 degrees, but 300 degrees may be okay depending on your oven.

4. Bake for 12 minutes and then take out to rotate the pan and shift the chips around a bit. Cook for another 12 minutes. In total, you should be baking them for about 25 minutes.

Salads

Picture inset: Red (Also Called Purple) Cabbage[7]

Hello Fall Salad

Traditional autumn vegetables are my favorite any time of the year, but from September to November I am constantly making these types of hearty salads. This salad can also be eaten raw.

<u>Ingredients</u> - Makes 2 servings
1 cup purple cabbage
2 beets
2-3 carrots, peeled
1 cup raw Brussels's Sprouts
1/2 cup walnuts (or pumpkin seeds!)
1 cup apples
1 cup butternut squash
(Optional) dressing of choice

Instructions for Beets

1. Wash, peel, and cut the edges of the beets off.
2. Puncture holes into them with a fork, wrap them in aluminum foil, and bake them at 400 degrees Fahrenheit.
3. Cooking time for beets varies by size. It should take anywhere from 40-60 minutes, so check back every so often.

Instructions for Squash

1. I buy fresh butternut squash, which can be notoriously difficult to open. In order to cut the squash, I put the squash in the microwave for 3-5 minutes to soften it up. However, use oven mitts when retrieving the squash as it will be very hot.
2. Slice the squash open lengthwise. With a spoon, scoop out the seeds and guts of the squash.
3. Place the squash on an oven rack and cook at 350 degrees Fahrenheit. The time it takes to cook the squash varies depending on its size. It should take anywhere from 40 to 60 minutes. I don't bother cutting the squash into cubes or peeling before hand as the skin comes off much easier when the squash has been cooked

General Instructions

1. Chop cabbage and Brussels's Sprouts very finely, so they are like shreds.
2. Peel carrots finely as well. This makes the "greens" of your salad.
3. Chop apples, beets, and walnuts up and add to the mix.
4. Finally, peel the butternut squash and cut into cubes.

Option: It is up to you whether or not to use dressing. I usually add nutritional yeast or lemon juice to this salad and that satisfies me rather than using anything with oil. The choice is yours. Something savory and nutty would be best for this salad.

Edamame Salad (Spicy)

This is by far one of my favorite go-to salads. I almost always have the ingredients in my house, and it takes about 10-15 minutes to make.

Ingredients (2 servings)

1 cup Edamame

2-3 cups spinach

1 large tomato or 20 cherry tomatoes

1-2 cups broccoli (Steamed or Raw)

Wegman's Organic Wasabi and Sriracha Sauce (Well, this is my favorite but feel free to mix it up a bit!)

Salt, Pepper

Juice of one lemon (2 tablespoons)

1 Avocado (Optional)

2 tablespoons Chia Seeds (Optional)

1. I buy frozen Edamame in bulk so I simply defrost a cup of them in the microwave.
2. Cut the tomatoes up into hearty chunks.
3. The broccoli may be eaten raw or steamed. I never sauté or use oil if I don't have to, though that is also an option. You can also fry with water or vegetable broth.

Options: As you can see, I have my favorite sauce. Feel free to make your own, or choose one of your own. A spicy sauce works very well with this salad. I will add avocado when I have it in the house, but it is not necessary.

Avocado & Mango Salad

This is a refreshing and filling summer salad. The creamy, savory avocado meshes well with the tarty, juicy mango. Enjoy!

<u>Ingredients</u> - Makes 2 servings

1 avocado

1 large mango (Any mango variety will do. It just depends on whether you want sweet or tart)

4 cups of greens, your choice - kale, spinach, and mixed greens work well. I do not suggest arugula.

3/4 cup Fresh Cilantro

2/3 cup of tomatoes

Salsa or Dressing (Optional)

No cooking required here! Enjoy this raw salad. I tend to not use dressing on my salads unless they are homemade. Instead I use spices, natural juices (lemon, lime), or homemade dips like salsa, hummus, and guacamole. I also love sprinkling some nutritional yeast onto my salads. It gives them a savory, almost cheesy flavor.

Soup & Stews

Vegan Tom Yum Soup (Spicy)

For the Stock

The most traditional Tom Yum soups include lemongrass, kaffir lime leaves, fish sauce, and a Thai root called Galangal. For vegans' and convenience's sake, this recipe does not include the fish sauce and substitutes Galangal for ginger. (You may also use Tamarind). You may be able to find galangal in your grocery store, but if you don't plan on using galangal much, ginger or tamarind will do just fine.

Ingredients - Makes 3-4 servings

5 cups vegetable stocks

2 stalks of lemon grass (I find this in the "Asian" produce section of my grocery store. It is in the produce section)

4 Kaffir Limes Leaves

1-2 teaspoon fresh, peeled, and chopped ginger (You can use ginger spice as well if fresh ginger is not available)

Juice of one lime (2 tablespoons)

1/2 teaspoon of cilantro

2 cloves of garlic

Either 2-3 minced green chili Peppers or 1-2 tablespoon chili paste

1/2 cup sweet onion minced

Instructions

The stock should left to boil on its own before adding any of the ingredients.

Instructions

1. Place 3 tablespoons of vegetable broth in a pot and add the chopped onions, crushed garlic, meatless ground crumbles, and chopped peppers to it. Watch the broth closely, and add more if necessary. The ground crumbles (if frozen) should be allowed to soften and defrost for about 10 minutes. If you are using the non-frozen ground crumbles it will take 5-8 minutes instead.

2. Then, add the vegetable stock, tomato paste, and the diced tomatoes.

3. Add the spices.

4. Let the spices and broth brew for at least 15-20 minutes before adding the beans and corn to the mix.

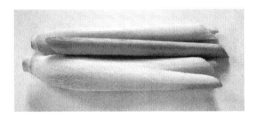

Picture inset: Prepared Lemon Grass[8]

Instructions For the Lemongrass

The lemon grass comes in stalks. Like you would with asparagus, cut off the white, hard portion so that the green stalk remains. You will cut it off again at the point where the leaves begin to grow from the stalk. Thus, you only need to use the main stalk. Continue cutting any portions that are not tender. Like an onion, remove the layers that are rough. Finally, when you have just the tender part of the lemon grass chop it into tiny pieces.

Picture inset: Kaffir Lime (Citrus Hystrix)[9]

For the Kaffir Lime Leaves

Simply remove the leaves from the stems and chop them finely. Once the soup is boiling, add the lime, kaffir lime leaves, lemon grass, onions, garlic, ginger, sugar, and chili paste (or peppers).

Add in the following:

2 Tomatoes (sliced)
2 cups of bok choy (Also called Asian cabbage) You will find this in any grocery sore
1 pack of firm tofu
1 cup mushrooms of choice (I like baby Portobello)

1. Chop tofu and mushrooms up and add to broth for 5-10 minutes.
2. Then, add the tomatoes and the bok choy. Let all the ingredients simmer for a few more minutes.
3. Add more spices, sugar, and soy sauce to prefect the taste. Serve with a soup ladle and enjoy!

Side note: Tom Yum is not supposed to be a thick soup or stew. More often than not it is part of a meal. You may want to include a side of rice or add noodles to your soup. You may thicken it up by using Coconut Milk. Tom Yum using Coconut Milk is Tom Kha Gai.

Cozy up Chili

This is a staple in my home during the cold winter months. I often make large servings and freeze it.

<u>Ingredients</u> - Makes 3-4 servings

1 large can diced tomatoes (about 28 oz.)

1 package of Morningstar, Boca Burger, or Yves Meatless Ground Crumbles (Made with TVP)

1 15.5 oz can of dark red kidney beans

1 15.5 oz can of black beans

3 tablespoon tomato paste

1.5 cup corn

1 cup & 3 tablespoons vegetable stock

1/2 cup chopped onions

3 garlic cloves

2 tablespoon chili powder

1 tablespoon cilantro

1 tablespoon cumin

1 red bell pepper

1 yellow bell pepper

1 green bell pepper

1-2 jalapeños, if desired

5. Let everything simmer on low-medium heat for another 15-20 minutes or so before serving.

Options: You can cook with olive oil instead of broth, include more or fewer jalapeños, or try making your own fake ground crumbles using tempeh, tofu, or softened walnuts that have been pureed in the food processor.

Picture inset: Gujarati Dahl[10]

Quintessential Dahl

Dahl is a traditional Indian and Nepalese staple made from lentils. In Nepal the dish dahl that is often consumed twice a day! The consistency of dahl varies from soupy to almost like a dip. This recipe creates a dahl that is somewhere between the two extremes. It can be eaten like a stew or it can be used as a dip for Pita or Naan bread.

Ingredients - Makes 2-3 servings

1 cup lentils

2.5 cups water or vegetable broth (adjust so the lentils and ingredients don't burn if this is not enough water for you)

2 tablespoons broth for the onion and cloves

1 teaspoon cumin

1 teaspoon turmeric

2 garlic cloves

1/2 teaspoon gram masala

Juice of one 1 lime (2 tablespoons)

1/2 cup onion

1 bay leaf

1 cup frozen spinach

Serve with rice, pita bread, or Naan bread.

Instructions

1. Wash the lentils and then pour them into the 2.5 cups of already boiling water or vegetable broth.

2. Let them simmer in the boiling water for 20 minutes or until soft.

3. Immediately after placing the lentils in the boiling water, add the spices.

4. Place 1 to 2 tablespoons of vegetable broth in a separate pan and let it simmer for a few moments before adding chopped onions and garlic. Simmer for 5-10 minutes.

5. Add the garlic and onion to the rest of the ingredients. Let all the ingredients simmer on low heat for another 10 minutes or so before servings.

Option: You can use various types of lentils (Yellow, read, green etc.). I prefer the green for this recipe, but the choice is yours.

Sandwiches

I'm including sandwiches in this recipe book because I get the question, "What do you eat for lunch?" so often, especially by colleagues. I don't take a sandwich to work every day as I really enjoy salads and Buddha bowls, but when I do I tend to impress my colleagues. Suddenly they wish they could trade their ham and cheese for a dill chickpea salad sandwich!

I am also including these recipes for parents raising vegetarian, vegan, or health-conscious children. Sandwiches make an easy, portable and mess-free lunch for little ones.

Choice of Bread

For these recipes choose whatever brand of bread you prefer, whether it is gluten-free or not. I would highly suggest you make or buy the most unprocessed, organic, whole-grain products at your disposal. Stay away from the major bread retailer's as they may add processed sugar, artificial preservatives, and oils.

Here are some of my favorite bread brands

Food for Life Baking Company - they are

vegan, organic, use no flour, are non-GMO, include no added sugar, and use no artificial preservatives. They have several different product lines to choose from and a wide variety of flavors. Their cinnamon raisin English muffins, in particular, are my favorites![11]

Manna Organics - they offer vegan, organic, non-GMO, and gluten-free breads free of added salt, oils, and sweeteners.[12]

Rudi's Organic Bakery - they offer vegan, organic, non-GMO and gluten-free bread products. They are also free of any artificial ingredients.[13]

Picture inset: Avocado Toast (with Cumin)[14]

Avocado & Chia Seed Toasties

This recipe is more of an open-faced sandwich snack than the type you can wrap up and take to work or school with you. If you wanted to make it a more substantial meal you could add more vegetables (cucumbers, sprouts, baby spinach, etc.) or baked tempeh slices. I also enjoy eating this for a filling breakfast or brunch.

Ingredients - Makes 1 full sandwich, 2 servings of toast
1/2 ripe avocado
2 slices of toast
1/4 teaspoon salt
4 slices tomato or cherry tomatoes
1 teaspoon chia seeds
Pepper to taste

1/4 teaspoon lemon juice

<u>Instructions</u>

1. Cut up the avocado and put half away for a later time.
2. Place the slices of avocado on top of the toast. It is up to you whether or not you want to spread them in or not. I like to leave it as is.
3. Place the tomato on top of the avocado.
4. Sprinkle salt, pepper, and chia seeds on top. Squeeze just the tiniest bit of lemon juice over the toast.

Dill Chickpea Salad Sandwich

I can't emphasize enough how much I love this dish. I probably make it at least once a month and bring it to work. The recipe takes 10 minutes to prepare and lasts you a few days.

Ingredients for the Chickpea filling - Makes 2-3 servings

1 can chickpeas

1.5 tablespoon Vegenaise

2 teaspoons dill weed

Pinch of cumin

Salt and pepper to taste

1-2 teaspoons organic, all natural Dijon mustard

Toppings/Add-Ons

2 slices tomatoes

Romaine Lettuce

Two pieces of bread

Instructions

1. Combine all of the chickpea filing ingredients in a food processor. You can also use a blender but you will have to stop periodically to squash some of the chickpeas back down to the blade.

2. Process on low power. You don't want the chickpeas to become puree. The finished product should resemble chicken salad. In essence, the chickpeas should be broken up and the spices and condiments should be evenly distributed. You should be able to see the chunks.

3. Grab two pieces of bread. Place sliced tomatoes and lettuce on bread first and then scoop chickpea salad onto the bread. Give yourself a generous portion.

Optional: You can add other toppings like avocado, sprouts, carrots, or hummus. You can also try substituting Vegenaise for another fat/thickening agent like avocado or tahini sauce. Just be aware that it will change the flavor and texture of the dish.

Portobello Mushroom Sandwich with Pesto, Roasted Red Peppers, and Spinach

Ingredients for the Portobello - Makes 1 serving

1 Portobello mushroom cap

1 tablespoon balsamic vinaigrette

Salt and pepper to taste

Instructions for the Portobello

1. To cook the Portobello Mushroom, preheat your oven to 425 degrees Fahrenheit.

2. Place aluminum foil on baking tray and place Portobello Mushroom on top of it.

3. Roast the mushroom for about 15 minutes, then check the progress. The mushroom should have shrunk a little and browned but it should not be dried out. Most of the balsamic vinaigrette will have been absorbed or cooked off, but you will likely have some run off.

Ingredients for the Roasted Red Peppers

3 Red Bell Peppers

<u>Instructions for the Roasted Red Peppers</u> - Makes 4 servings

1. Cut the stem off the bell peppers and cut the bell peppers in half.
2. Remove the seeds and the inside contents.
3. Place the pepper face down on a baking sheet with aluminum foil.
4. Cook at 450 degrees Fahrenheit for 20 minutes.
5. Check on the peppers after 20 minutes. The skin should be charred on most of its surface. You may have to cook them for an additional 10 minutes.

Picture inset: Pesto sauce[15]

You can either buy organic, unprocessed pesto or you can make your own if you have a decent food processor. Below is a simple pesto recipe.

Pesto Sauce

<u>Ingredients for the Pesto</u> - Makes 8 servings

Some oil is necessary to maintain the consistency and texture of the pesto. A little oil goes a long way.

2 cups fresh basil

3 cloves garlic

3 tablespoons olive oil

2 tablespoons vegetable broth

Salt and pepper to taste

Juice of half a lemon (1 tablespoon)

1/4 cup walnuts

1/4 parsley

Instructions for Pesto

1. Place all ingredients into a food processor and puree until smooth yet chunky.
2. The pesto should not be runny. It should be thick, but easily spreadable.

Final Steps to Complete the Sandwich

1. Spread a dollop of pesto on each side of your bread.
2. After you have let the roasted bell peppers cool for at least ten minutes, cut them into thick slices and place a few on your bread.
3. Then, place the mushroom on top of one side of your bread.
4. Put the rest of the pesto and roasted red peppers

in storage containers and place in the fridge for later use.

Note: This does not always make the best sandwich to bring to lunch, unless you are putting it on a very hard bread (i.e. Ciabatta).

Grown-Up Grilled Peanut Butter & Fruit Sandwich

Peanut Butter should be more of a rare indulgence in my house than it actually is. But, I carefully purchase the all-natural, organic peanut butter and limit it two tablespoons (8 grams protein). Peanut Butter also has a substantial source of essential omega-6 fatty acids. Sometimes all I really want is a peanut butter sandwich and it's great knowing that peanut butter in moderation can be good for me!

So, here's a gourmet, grown-up, and of course, vegan recipe for the perfect peanut butter sandwich.

Ingredients - Makes 1 serving

2 tablespoons of all-natural, non-GMO, no sugar-added, peanut butter

2 slices of toast

4 sliced strawberries

2 teaspoons Nutella or other Hazelnut Spread

1-2 teaspoons shredded, unsweetened coconut

1 bananas, chopped

Dollop of coconut oil

Instructions

1. Spread one tablespoon of peanut butter onto each slice of bread.

2. Optional - Spread one teaspoon of Nutella on each side of toast on top of the peanut butter

3. Then, chop up your banana into half inch slices and place them evenly across both pieces of toast.

4. Wash and peel the leaves off the strawberries. Cut them lengthwise three or four times and place them on the bread.

5. To grill my bread I usually use a toaster oven or my panini maker since it doesn't need oil.

However, if you do not have one of these items you can always grill it in a skillet. To do so, spread about one tablespoon worth of coconut oil on a pan. Put the sandwich together and cook each side for about 3 minutes. Enjoy!

Main Meals

This chapter is organized into several different sections based on what the meal's bulk ingredients are. The section includes grain-based, nut-based, legume-based, soy-based, and vegetable-based meals.

Grain-Based

Stuffed Peppers

Ingredients - Makes 2 servings, plus leftover filling

2 Bell Peppers (any color)

1/3 Cup Dry Quinoa, Brown Rice, or Farro

1 15.5 oz can of black beans (roughly one pound)

1 teaspoon cumin

1 garlic clove

1-2 tablespoons water

1 teaspoon chili powder

1/2 teaspoon cilantro

1/2 cup onion chopped

1/2 tablespoon olive oil

1/2 cup soy cheese (optional)

Avocado (optional)

Instructions for the filling

1.   In a skillet, heat 2 tablespoons of water.

2. Add onions on medium-high heat and cook, stirring occasionally, until they soften.

3. Combine cooked rice (1/3 cup of dry rice makes a little over one cup cooked) and the black beans to the onions. Add spices and let them simmer on low-heat for a few minutes to absorb some of the flavor.

Instructions for the peppers

1. Wash two bell peppers and cut a wide circle around the stem (As you would carve a pumpkin).

2. Remove the stem (Some twisting may be required). Use a spoon or fork to get rid of the seeds of the pepper. Then, add the rice and beans mix equally to each pepper. Depending on the size of the pepper, you'll probably have extra.

3. If you'd like to have soy or rice cheese, add the cheese on top of the beans and rice now.

4. Bake in oven at 375 degrees Fahrenheit for about 20 minutes or so, or until the cheese has melted and the skin of the pepper starts to peel and brown a little bit.

Picture inset: Stuffed Acorn Squash[16]

Fall, Flavorful Stuffed Acorn Squash

<u>Ingredients</u> - Makes 4 servings

2 acorn squash

1/2 cup raisins

1 cup garbanzo beans

2 carrots

1 cup vegetable broth or water

1 cup couscous

1/2 cup sliced dates

1/4 cup walnuts

1 teaspoon gram masala

1 teaspoon ginger

1 tablespoon brown sugar

Instructions for Squash

1. Cut the squash in half vertically. If it is difficult to cut, then put it in the microwave for a few minutes to warm it up for easier cutting.

2. After cutting it open, use a spoon to clean out the loose pulp and seeds. Take a knife and make checkmark/cross-hatch cuts inside both halves of the squash.

3. Preheat the oven to 375 to 400 degrees Fahrenheit.

4. Place the two halves in a pan with just enough water that it covers the bottom of the pan.

5. Place the two halves face up. Cook for one hour, and occasionally check. See if they are tender with a fork. When you can pierce the squash easily with a fork, they are ready to be eaten.

Instructions for Filling

1. Bring the water to a boil and then add the couscous.

2. It takes roughly 10 minutes for the couscous to absorb the water. Fluff the couscous up with a fork so it keeps a soft and airy consistency.

3. Pour garbanzo beans, raisins, sliced dates, peeled and chopped carrots, and chopped walnuts into the mix. Stir, then add the spices.

General Instructions

1. When the acorn squash is nearly done (perhaps 5 more minutes) take it out and put the filling in the two halves. You may have some extra to save as leftovers.

2. Place back in the oven and cook for 5 more minutes.

Nut-Based Recipes

Broccoli Alfredo Pasta (Made with Cashews)

This recipe requires a food processor or a very strong blender.

Ingredients - Makes 6 servings

8oz. pasta of your choice

2 cups chopped broccoli

Ingredients for the Alfredo Sauce - Makes 6 servings

1/3 cup cashews (unsalted)

1 garlic clove

Pepper to taste

1 cup vegetable stock or non-dairy milk

Juice of one lemon (2 tablespoons)

3 tablespoons nutritional yeast

1 tablespoon Tahini

1 teaspoon soy sauce/tamari sauce

Instructions

1. Steam the broccoli and boil the pasta separately.

2. Blend all of the ingredients for the cashew Alfredo sauce together until smooth.
3. Combine pasta, broccoli, and sauce together in a large bowl.
4. Stir so that sauce is evenly distributed amongst the pastas and broccoli. Enjoy!

Picture inset: Gado-Gado Ingredient Stall in Indonesia[17]

Vegan Gado-Gado

Gado-Gado is one of my favorite dishes, so I am excited to share it. This dish is a traditional, peanut-based Indonesian dish. It is a hearty salad that usually contains hard-boiled eggs, fried tofu or tempeh, potatoes, and a medley of vegetables (often bean sprouts, spinach, cabbage, corn). A thick, savory peanut sauce is spread over it. This is a vegan adaptation of that meal, so I don't include the eggs in this dish.

Ingredients for Peanut Sauce - Makes 8 servings
3/4 cup all-natural, organic, no-sugar added crunch peanut butter
1 cup non-dairy milk
1 tablespoon soy sauce
3 tablespoons sugar (date, coconut are best) or 2

tablespoons agave syrup

1 teaspoon chili powder or chili flakes

Juice of 1 lime (2 tablespoons)

  tablespoon nutritional yeast

Instructions

Blend or put in food processor on high power until smooth. The sauce should be on the thicker side, but still serve as a dressing. Adjust liquid and dry ingredients accordingly.

Ingredients for Tempeh - Makes 3 servings

(I bake my tempeh, and use no oil)

One block of tempeh

Salt

Pepper

Instructions for Tempeh

1. Cut tempeh up into small, equal-sized blocks.
2. Preheat oven to 350 degrees Fahrenheit and cook for 20 minutes.
3. Turn the tempeh over half way through so it does not burn.

<u>Ingredients for Vegetables</u> - Makes 3 servings

1 cups bean sprouts

1 large cucumber

1 cup bok choy

2 Beefsteak tomatoes

2 cups Purple Cabbage

<u>Instructions for Vegetables</u>

All of this can be eaten raw, though you might want to boil the bok choy first before adding it to the meal. Bok Choy only needs to be boiled for a few minutes.

<u>Potatoes</u> - Makes 3 servings

2-3 medium-sized potatoes

1. Cut up the potatoes into large chunks and boil them until tender.
2. Add the tempeh, potatoes, and vegetables together. Pour peanut sauce over the dish and enjoy!

Soy-Based Recipes

Sloppy Joe's with Baked Oil-Free Sweet Potato Fries

While vegetarian Sloppy Joe's are marginally better for you than the meat version, they are delicious. This dish is a perfect way to serve any picky eaters or non-vegans out there that may balk at tofu or bright vegetables. It is a great, quick meal for children as well.

Base Ingredients

6 all-natural, whole-wheat or gluten free hamburger buns

1 package of TVP (textured vegetable protein) meatless ground beef

Instructions for the Sauce - Makes 6 servings

1/4 cup unprocessed sugar, preferable coconut, date or brown sugar

1/2 cup onion chopped

2 cups plain tomato sauce

2 tablespoons tomato paste

2 tablespoons nutritional yeast

1 teaspoons cinnamon

1 medium-sized carrot, peeled and minced

1 table spoon Worcestershire sauce (make sure it is labeled vegan)

2 cloves garlic

1 teaspoon chili powder (optional)

1/4 cup water (optional)

Instructions

1. Bring the tomato sauce to a low boil in a pan.

2. Add the rest of the ingredients, including the fake meat to the pan and simmer for about 15 minutes, or until the fake meat has defrosted and the vegetables have tenderized.

3. Serve on a toasted bun

Sweet Potato Fries - Makes 6 servings

5 Sweet Potatoes

2 tablespoons dates, coconut, or brown sugar

Instructions

1. Preheat the oven to 400 degrees Fahrenheit.

2. Clean and scrub the dirt off the sweet potatoes.

3. Cut into slices no more than a half inch thick.

4. Place parchment paper on a tray and spread the fries evenly over the surface.

5. Coat the fries with the sugar (or you can use

salt and pepper). Cook about 20 minutes, turning over once.

Picture inset: Tempeh in Chili Sauce[18]

Tempeh Lettuce Tacos

Ingredients - Makes 3 servings

1 package plain tempeh

3 teaspoons cumin

2 teaspoons cilantro

2-3 teaspoon chili powder

1/2 chopped onion

1 tablespoon olive oil

1 teaspoon paprika

1/2 cup tomatoes

1 clove garlic

3 Romaine lettuce hearts (Or one for each taco you make)

Optional Toppings

Salsa

Guacamole

Jalapeno peppers

Instructions for filling

1. On medium-high heat, cook 1 tablespoon olive oil on a skillet and add chopped onion and garlic. Let the onion and garlic cook on their own for a few minutes. Add more water if needed.

2. Preparing the tempeh is simple. Simply break the tempeh up into large blocks and then crumble it into a large bowl to collect all of it. Tempeh is quite hard, unlike tofu, so crumbling comes easily.

3. Add the spices to the tempeh and then put the ingredients into the skillet. Add extra oil or vegetable broth if needed.

4. The tempeh is almost done when the edges get crispy. This should take around 10 minutes.

5. Add the tomatoes about 7-10 minutes in, depending on how quickly your tempeh is cooking.

6. Take romaine lettuce hearts and separate them to make "taco shells."

7. They can be large so it may necessary to trim the lettuce to make the shells.

8. Pile the tempeh filling into the lettuce shells and then add toppings of your choice on top of it.

9. Possible toppings include: salsa, guacamole, chili peppers, olives, or shredded soy cheese.

Legume-Based Recipes

Picture inset: Falafel[19]

Oil-Free, Baked Falafels

(Inspired by Plant-Based Judy)[20]

Ingredients for Falafels - Makes about small 12-16 falafels

1 15.5 oz can chickpeas

1 cup chickpea flour

2 cloves garlic

1 teaspoon cumin

2 teaspoon cilantro

1 teaspoon turmeric

fresh parsley

Juice of one lemon (2 tablespoons)

1/2 cup red onion

Instructions

1. Preheat the oven to 350 degrees Fahrenheit.

2. Using a food processor or strong blender, mince garlic, onion, and parsley.

3. Then add the rest of your ingredients into the food processor or blender and continue until everything starts sticking together.

4. Set parchment paper down on racks so that the falafel doesn't stick.

5. Either scoop or use your hands to make small 2 inch balls. Press down on them lightly so they are more oval than circular.

6. Cook for 15-20 minutes on one side. Then, take them out of the oven and turn them over. Don't worry if some of the falafel stick to the parchment paper.

7. Put them back in the oven for 5-10 minutes more. Pull them out and let them dry at least 10 minutes before transferring them.

8. You can eat these as a snack, put them on a salad, or make a pita falafel sandwich out of them. I tend to do all three, but they certainly don't last long!

Black Bean, Sweet Potato, and Kale Burgers

Ingredients for Black Bean Mix - Makes 6-8 burgers

One 15.5 oz can black beans (this is the typical size cans you find in your grocery store)

2 cups mashed sweet potato

1.5 cups brown rice (cooked) - roughly 1/3 dry brown rice

1 cup kale

2 teaspoons cumin

1 teaspoons paprika

1 clove garlic

1 teaspoon chili powder (optional)

Instructions for Sweet Potatoes

1. If I am in a rush I microwave the sweet potatoes until they are tender, but baking them gives them a better, more tender consistency.

2. To bake your sweet potatoes, preheat the oven to 400 degrees Fahrenheit and slice the potatoes in half and cook until they are tender. Depending on how large the potatoes are, they may need to bake about 40 minutes.

Instructions for Rice

1. Cook the rice while the sweet potatoes are cooking. Bring one and a quarter cup of water to a boil. Include a pinch of salt.
2. Add 1/3 cup dry rice and turn the heat down.
3. Cook for about 30 minutes for brown rice, and 20 for white rice depending on how quickly the water is absorbed.

Instructions for Kale

1. For the kale, rips the leaves from the stems and throw stems away.
2. Place and let the kale boil in water for about 5 minutes or until the kale is tender and soft. Remove and strain kale.
3. When cool, mince in a food processor or blender for 30 seconds.

General Instructions

1. Remove the skin from the sweet potatoes.
2. Add rice, potatoes, beans, kale, and spices into a large mixing bowl.
3. Using a potato masher is very helpful in this regard as well. Mix until the ingredients all stick together.

4. Turn the oven on to 350 degrees Fahrenheit. Place parchment paper on trays. With your hands or a scooper make mounds of burger and flatten just a bit. They should be a few inches in diameter.

5. Cook for 10 minutes or so on each side, possibly more. The outside should be crispy. The inside should be cooked, but still tender. Place fork in middle of the burger and see if anything comes up with the fork. It it does, it is not quite ready.

6. Serve on a bun or by itself and enjoy!

Vegetable-Based Recipes

Picture inset: Variation of Raw Zucchini Spaghetti[21]

Zucchini Spaghetti & Soy Meatballs

Ingredients - 2 Zucchinis make 1 serving

2 Zucchinis (Spiraled) – I usually do yellow and green to get in a variety

1/2 cup Tomato Sauce (Homemade or organic store bought)

3-6 Soy Meatballs (Depending on hunger!)

1/3 Cup fresh basil

Juice of one lemon (2 tablespoons)

For this recipe you will need a spiralizer. They almost always cost under $50, but you can get a very capable one for as low as $20.

Instructions

1. Cut the stem off of the zucchini.
2. Clean the zucchini and insert it into a spiralizer. Your spiralizer may be electric or manual. If it is the latter, some twisting of the zucchini may be required. When you use the spiralizer, strands of zucchini will come out that look exactly like spaghetti!
3. You can either buy tomato sauce at the store (make sure it is organic, low-sodium, with very few added sugars to it), or you can make your own. Below you will find a recipe I often use to make sauce:

Ingredients for Tomato Sauce - Makes 8 servings

6 oz can tomato paste

1-28 oz can crushed tomatoes

1-1.5 cups water, depending on how thick you want your sauce

1 chopped onion

3 cloves of garlic

2 teaspoon oregano

1 cup fresh basil

Salt and pepper to taste

1/2 tablespoon of lemon juice

Instructions for Tomato Sauce

1. Cook onion and garlic on skillet for a few minutes with two tablespoons water.

2. Blend together with the rest of the ingredients.

3. Sprinkle fresh basil on top of finished zucchini and sauce.

4. I use frozen soy meatballs for this recipe as it tends to be one of my go-to quick meals. However, feel free to take the initiative to make your own! They can be nut-based, soy-based, or legume-based. This is just a great instance of how meat-free alternatives opens up so many more options.

Buddha Bowl (Template)

A Buddha bowl can be anything you want it to be, as long as the bulk of it is made from vegetables with some healthy, whole-food protein and grains. Essentially, it is a flexible, customizable nutrient-rich meal. It's a meal you gather from whatever is left in your fridge.

I make these a lot when I have a few random vegetables, a serving or so of grains, and maybe just a few leftover falafels or one can of beans to my disposal.

Here is a template for a Buddha bowl. I'm not providing a specific recipe because the magic of a Buddha bowl is that you can make it to your liking!

First Step: Choose the Grain/Starch
Possible options are:

Sweet Potato, or any other variety potato (Purple, Red, Japanese Sweet Potato)

Couscous

Farro

Barley

Quinoa

Brown Rice

Noodles

Step Two: Choose your Protein

Protein Ideas:

Baked or Raw Tofu

Baked Tempeh

Garbanzo, Black, Kidney, Cannellini Beans

Edamame

Step Three: Toppings

Nuts, Seeds, and Other Goodies:

Flaxseed

Walnuts

Almonds

Pistachios

Chia Seeds

Nutritional Yeast

Roasted Red Peppers

Olives

Raw Granola

Sliced Apples

Raisins

Cranberries

Step four: Vegetables

Cauliflower

Broccoli

Carrots

Squash

Zucchini

Mushrooms

Tomatoes

Cucumbers

Step five: Leafy Greens

Kale

Collard Greens

Spinach

Romaine

Arugula

Put the Finishing Touches on it: Dressings/Sauce

Peanut Sauce

Tahini Sauce

Balsamic Vinaigrette

Salsa

Guacamole

Sriracha

Lemon & Tahini

Lemon Juice

Desserts

There are actually plenty of ways to substitute eggs and butter for vegan items. While many readers are probably familiar with applesauce for oil, readers may not be aware of flaxseed "eggs" or avocado for butter and other vegan baking tricks of the trade. This chapter provides readers with three essential desserts. Readers will learn about some of these substitutes and use them in their own cooking.

Picture inset: Vegan Brownie[22]

Vegan Flourless Brownies (Black beans you say?)

This recipe is inspired by Chocolate Covered Katie, the internet Queen of vegan baked goods. I simply had to include her in this recipe book one way or another.[23]

Ingredients

1 can black beans

3 tablespoons raw, unsweetened cocoa powder

1/2 cup quick oats (not the steel cut)

1/3 cup maple syrup, coconut sugar, or agave syrup

1/4 cup coconut oil or avocado

2 teaspoons vanilla

1/2 teaspoon baking powder

2/3 cup dark chocolate chips

Instructions

1. Preheat Oven to 350 degrees Fahrenheit.

2. Combine all ingredients (except the dark chocolate chips) into a large blender or food processor and blend thoroughly until the ingredients are smooth. It will be quite thick. Katie recommends a food processor highly over a blender, as the texture and consistency of the brownies will be much better. She says the taste is also quite different.

3. Pour the mixture onto a lightly greased 8x8 pan and add the chocolate chips on top. They should cook no longer than 15-18 minutes. You can let them sit in the fridge to firm up. It makes about a dozen brownies.

Healthy, Vegan, Gluten-Free Pecan Pumpkin Pie

Ingredients for the Crust

3/4 cup Pecans

2 cups flour (or a combination of oats, almond and coconut)

1/4 cup applesauce

1/2 cup pitted dates

2 tablespoons non-dairy milk

2 tablespoons coconut oil

Instructions for Crust

1. Blend the dry ingredients in a food processor for about 30 seconds until it is mixed.

2. Then add the rest of the crust ingredients and blend until fine and crumbly (it should be somewhat sticky though so if it is too dry add more milk).

3. Transfer the mixture onto a slightly greased pie plate. Flatten the mixture out with your hands and press it up against the edges of the pie pan so that it even across the pan. There should not be thin patches or holes anyway.

Ingredients for the Filling

1 can organic, unsweetened pumpkin puree

1/2 teaspoon all spice

1 teaspoons ginger

1 cup non-dairy milk

1/2 cup maple syrup

1 teaspoon cinnamon

1/4 teaspoon cloves

1 teaspoon vanilla

Instructions for the Filling

1. Place all of the filling ingredients in a blender and puree until smooth and even.

2. Pour the filling into the pie plate and place in the oven at 400 degrees Fahrenheit.

3. After 10 minutes or so, drop the temperature to 350 degrees Fahrenheit and bake for another 30 minutes, checking every so often on the state of the crust and the center of the pie.

4. When the crust is golden and the center looks mostly set, take the pie from the oven. It needs to be cooled completely, (either on a rack or in the fridge) before cutting and serving.

Picture inset: Vegan Nice Cream[24]

Vegan "Nice Cream" – So many options!

After trying nice cream once, you'll be hooked. You can make nice cream with just one, magical ingredient: Frozen Bananas, but adding multiple ingredients to this dish makes a tasty dessert absolutely scrumptious.

Instructions

1. To make nice cream, take at least 2 bananas and split them into chunk. You can use as many bananas as you like, but 2 bananas are a good start.

2. Freeze the bananas before using. I often buy a bunch in bulk, wait until they turn spotty and then freeze them for my nice cream.

3. When they are frozen, take out the desired

amount of bananas for nice cream. Four bananas is a nice amount, but depends on your hunger.

4. Put the bananas in a blender or food processor. The bananas will grind down and look a bit like flakes.

5. This is good. Like magic, when you add a teaspoon or two of non-dairy milk, the bananas will liquefy again and become a thick, creamy consistency, just like ice cream!

You can add all sorts of ingredients to your nice cream. Here are a list of my favorite options to add:

Chocolate −Peanut Butter Monster

2 tbsp cocoa

1.5 tbsp all natural, creamy peanut butter

2 teaspoons additional non-dairy milk

Green Protein-Power

1 heaping handful of spinach

2 tablespoons vegan protein powder

Top with mixed berries and chia seeds

Raspberry –Orange

2 navel oranges

1 cup raspberries

1 tbsp agave syrup may be needed

Tropical Nice Cream

1 mango

1/2 pineapple

Pistachio

1/4 cup finely chopped pistachios

1-2 tablespoons maple syrup

Strawberry Bananas

1 cup of strawberries, chopped

Cherry Dark Chocolate

1 cup bing cherries

2 tbsp cocoa

4 dates, pitted

Conclusion

I hope this book's recipes are flexible, easy to follow, and liked by vegans and non-vegans alike. I have consistently included alterations and adaptations to the book's recipes so readers with various taste buds and dietary lifestyles can enjoy them. The recipes in this book are organized. Each recipe includes separate ingredient lists and instructions for the recipes' main components. For example, instead of listing all the ingredients and instructions for zucchini pasta and tomato sauce at once, I separated the instructions for zucchini from the instructions for the sauce.

Finally, I hope this recipe book allows vegans to share their lifestyle with others, especially people who eat all that brown stuff. As this book's introduction stated, vegan cooking is much more about inclusivity than it is exclusivity. One way to make vegan recipes more inclusive is to design them in a way that non-vegans can enjoy them as well. Instead of scaring meat-eaters off with ingredients like Spirulina and Maca Powder, this book includes ingredients we all grew up enjoying like bananas, sweet potatoes, warm chili, and even peanut butter sandwiches!

Thank You

Thank you for downloading my book and I hope you enjoyed it and found many things insightful. Furthermore, you can opt-in to my Book Notification Group to get all the latest information on free promotions, discounts and future book releases. Go to http://eepurl.com/bfE46z to get signed up.

I would really appreciate if you would take a minute to post a review on Amazon about this book. I check all my reviews and love to get feedback (this is the real reward for me - knowing that I'm helping others).

If you have any friends or family that may enjoy this book, please spread the love and gift it to them.

View my other work at Amazon Author Central.

About the Author

Lewis Haas is a father of 3 girls and a freelance writer. He enjoys daily meditation, exercising and spending time with his family. Currently residing in Tampa, Florida, his favorite time of year is winter when he meditates in the great outdoors.

References

[1] King, 2015

[2] Tofu Scramble, 2008.

[3] Parenting Patch, 2013

[4] Bodzioch, 2011

[5] Easy Vegan Granola, 2012

[6] Kale Chips. (2009, April 9). Retrieved from https://commons.wikimedia.org/wiki/File:Kale_Chips_(3425805140).jpg

[7] Biusch, 2012.

[8] Morley, 2005.

[9] Mokkie, 2014.

[10] Vyas, 2008.

[11] Food For Life Baking Company. (2015). Retrieved from http://www.foodforlife.com

[12] Manna Organics: Sprouted for Life. (n.d.) Retrieved from http://www.mannaorganicbakery.com

[13] Rudi's Organic Bakery. (n.d.) Retrieved from http://www.rudisbakery.com

[14] Palmero, 2015.

[15] Pesto, 2007.

[16] Sessmus, 2014.

[17] Mitori 2009.

[18] Midori, 2011.

[19] Falafel Balls, 2009.

[20] Plant Based Judy, 2014.

[21] Sietske, 2013.

[22] Suzette, 2012.

[23]Chocolate Covered Katie, 2012.

[24] Allin Para, n.d.

Resources

>Allin Parasa. n.d. Vegan Ice Cream: Smashed Frozen Banana with Saffron. [Image] Retrieved from http://commons.wikimedia.org/wiki/ File:Ailin24VeganIceCream.JPG

>Biusch. (2012, November 3).   Red Cabbage; half sliced, cross section. [Image] Retrieved from https://commons.wikimedia.org/wiki/File:Red_cabb age.tiff

>Bodzioch, Simon. (2011, July 10). Löwenzahn-Smoothie. [Image] Retrieved from https://commons.wikimedia.org/wiki/File:Löwenza hn-Smoothie.jpg

>Chickpeas Salad Sandwich with Chunky Chopped Chickpea Salad, Sliced Cucumbers, Roasted Red Peppers, and Onion Confit. [Image] (2010, January

11). Retrieved from
https://commons.wikimedia.org/wiki/
File:Chickpea_salad_sandwich_-_01.jpg
>Chocolate Covered Katie (2012, September 6). No
Flour Black Bean Brownies.
[Blog Post] Retrieved from
http://chocolatecoveredkatie.com/2012/09/06/no-flo
ur-black-bean-brownies/
>Easy Vegan Granola. (2012, February 21). [Image]
Retrieved from
https://commons.wikimedia.org/wiki/File:Easy_Ve
gan_Granola_(6781445588).jpg
>Falafel Balls. (2009). [Image] Retrieved from
http://commons.wikimedia.org/wiki/
File:Falafel_balls.jpg
>King, Barbara. (2015, March 12). "Does Being
Vegan Really Help Animals?" *NPR.* Retrieved from
http://www.npr.org/sections/13.7/2015/03/12/39247
9865/does-being-vegan-really-help-animals
>Liddon, Angela. (2011,   January 3). Quick and
Easy Vegan Alfredo. Retrieved from
http://ohsheglows.com/2011/01/03/quick-and-easy-
vegan-alfredo/
>Mokkie. (2014, March 31). Kaffir Lime (Citrus
Hystrix). [Image] Retrieved from

https://commons.wikimedia.org/wiki/File:Kaffir_Lime_(Citrus_hystrix).jpg

>Morley, Malcom.(2005, December). Prepared Lemon Grass. [Image] Retrieved from https://commons.wikimedia.org/wiki/File:Prepared_lemon_grass.JPG

>Midori, Sakurai. (2009, July 10). Gado-Gado Stall at a Traditional Market in Jakarta. [Image] Retrieved from http://commons.wikimedia.org/wiki/File:Gado-Gado_stall.JPG

>Midori. (2011, July 31). Tempeh in Chili Sauce. [Image] Retrieved from http://commons.wikimedia.org/wiki/File:Sambal_goreng_tempe.JPG

>Palmero, Nan. (2015, March 22). Rosella Coffeeshop Avocado Toast with Cumin [Image] Retrieved from https://commons.wikimedia.org/wiki/

>File:Rosella_Coffeeshop_Avocado_Toast_with_Cumin_-_North_River_District,_San_Antonio,_Texas_(2015-03-22_by_Nan_Palmero).jpg

>Parenting Patch. (2013). Cup of Chia Seed Pudding. [Image]. Retrieved from

https://commons.wikimedia.org/wiki/File:Cup_of_
Chia_Seed_Pudding.jpg

>Pesto. (2007, October 20). [Image] Retrieved from
https://commons.wikimedia.org/wiki/File:Making_
pesto.jpg

>Plant Based Judy. (2014, September 28). Oil-Free
Falafel. [Video] Retrieved from
https://www.youtube.com/watch?v=wAVFEI2gnPg

>Sessmus, Christopher. (2014, November 16.
Squash V. [Image] Retrieved from
http://commons.wikimedia.org/wiki/File:Cucurbita
_pepo_Acorn_squash_-_Squash_V.jpg

>Sietske. (2013, August 31). Spaghetti made from
Zucchini, served in an Antwerp Lunchroom
following the raw foodism principle. [Image]
Retrieved from
http://commons.wikimedia.org/wiki/File:Falafel_ba
lls.jpg

>Suzette. (2012, March 1). Vegan Brownie.
[Image[Retrieved from
http://commons.wikimedia.org/wiki/File:Vegan_br
ownie_(6944564463).jpg Tofu >Scramble. [Image]
(2008, March 31). Retrieved from
http://commons.wikimedia.org/wiki/File:Tofu_scr.j
pg

>Vyas, Dhaval, S. (2008, March 30). Gujarati Daal (Soup) made of Tuver Dal (Split Cajanus Cajun) [Image] Retrieved from https://commons.wikimedia.org/wiki/File:Gujarati_daal.jpg

Made in the USA
Middletown, DE
06 December 2017